A Mother's Love

Written by Elpida Marangou
Illustrated by Sarah K. Turner

Halo
PUBLISHING
INTERNATIONAL

ISBN: 978-1-63765-060-8
LCCN: 2021911703

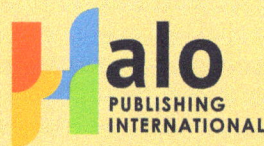

Halo Publishing International, LLC
www.halopublishing.com

Printed and bound in the United States of America

I dedicate this to book to
all mothers and my children—

Mitchell, Meagan, Mason

You will always feel my love wrapped around you
like a blanket of sunshine on a sunny, sunny day.

Soar my little ones! For my love will soar with you.

I love you – from your head to your toes,
from your knees to your nose,
from your eyes to your ears
and your itty-bitty mouth.

I loved you yesterday.

I love you today and tomorrow
and forever and a day from the stars
above and to the moon and back.

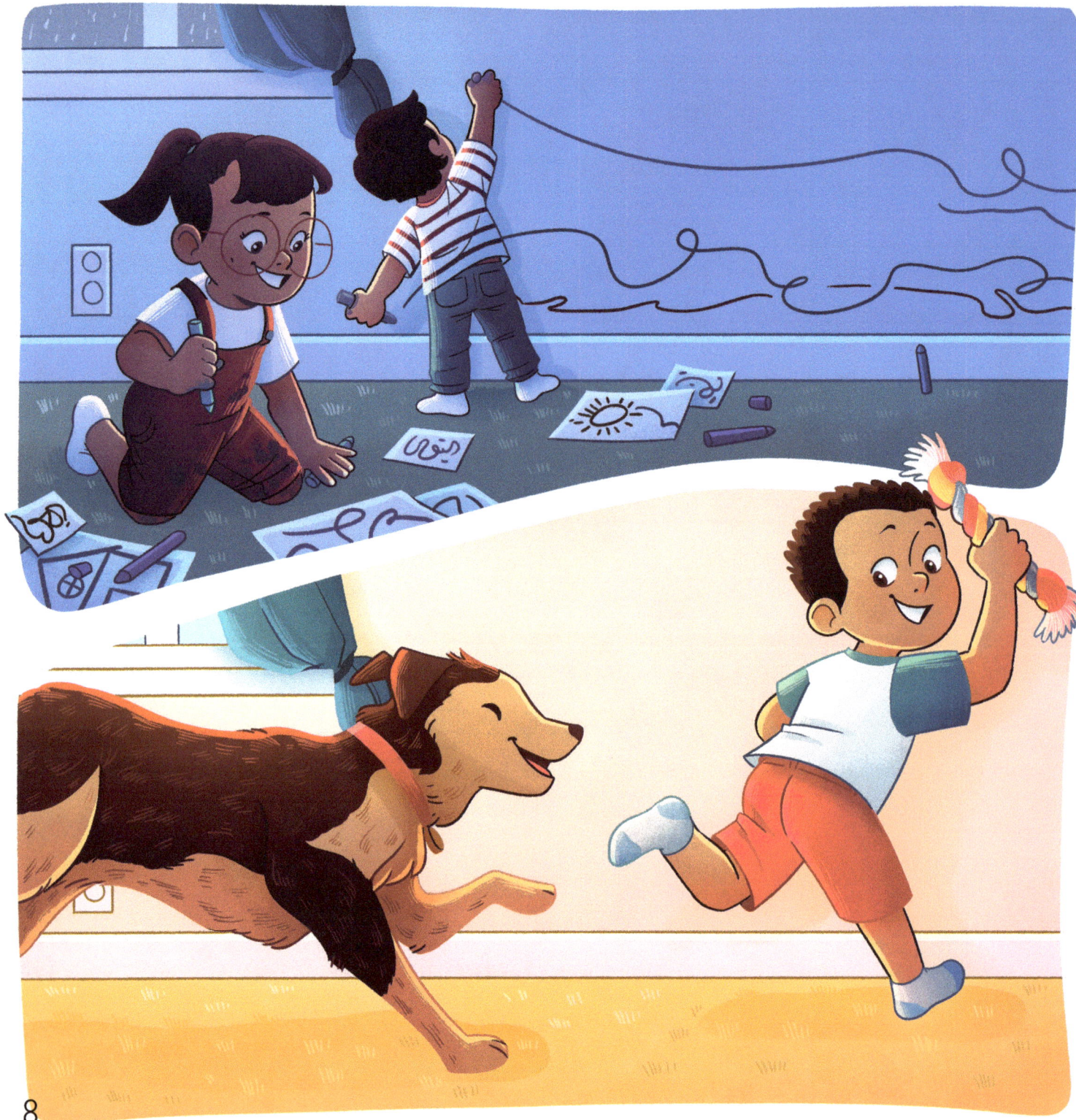

I love you from the darkest
nights to the brightest days.

My love is wrapped around you
like a blanket of sunshine
on a sunny, sunny day.

My love is bountiful, but it will be
challenged when you make a spill, throw
food on the floor or even color the walls.
"No matter," I say. "You will stop that someday."

I love you when you splash in muddy puddles wearing your brand-new shoes.

What fun you are having!

"Oh no!"

"Who cares?"

I say. "I will wash them anyway!"

I love you just the way you are.

I love you— upside down or down side up;
one-handed, two-handed, ten fingers and ten toes;
one-footed, two-footed, three-footed or more;
left-footed, right-footed, one socked or unmatched!

"No matter!" I say. "For I love you that way."

I love you when you go this way
and that way, when we're heading out
the door, sitting, standing or rolling
downhill; singing, laughing, happy or sad.

"No matter, my child, I love our
time together each and every day."

No feet, no hands, one hand, or two,
cross-eyed or a pirate's eye—

"No matter!" I say. "For, you're cute that way."

A witch's nose, a freckle, a scar, does not matter,
you see, for you bring love to me so easily.

From my head to my toes, from my knees to my nose,
from my eyes to my ears and my big smiling mouth,
you will always feel my love wrapped around you
like a blanket of sunshine on a sunny, sunny day.

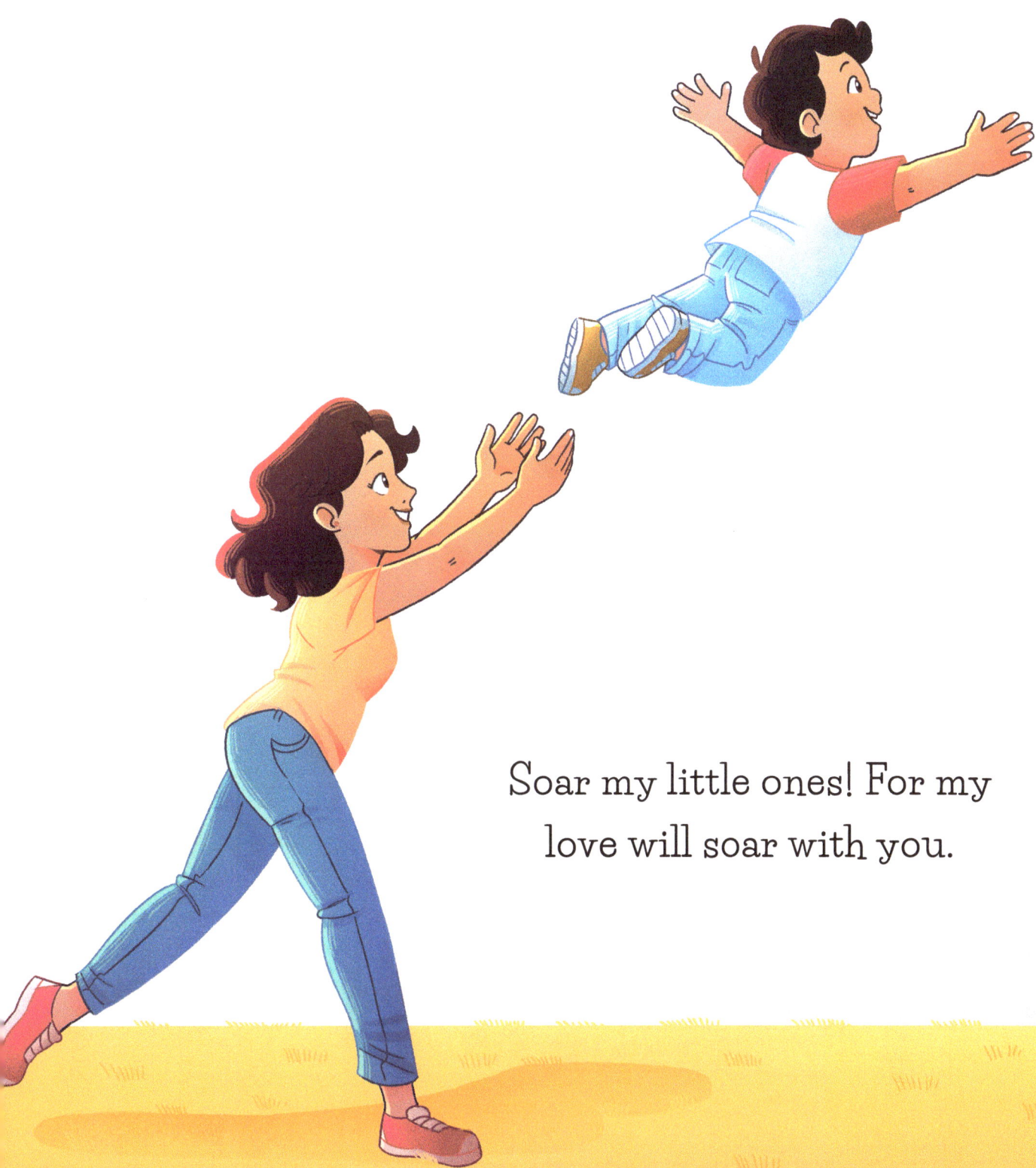

Soar my little ones! For my love will soar with you.